I WONDER Why

Triceratops Had Horns

and other questions
about dinosaurs

Rod Theodorou

KINGFISHER
NEW YORK

First published 1994 by Kingfisher
This edition published 2011 by Kingfisher

Distributed in the U.S. by Macmillan, 175 Fifth Ave.,
New York, NY 10010
Distributed in Canada by H.B. Fenn and Company Ltd.,
34 Nixon Road, Bolton, Ontario L7E 1W2

Library of Congress Cataloging-in-Publication data has been
applied for.

ISBN 978-0-7534-6554-7 (HC)
ISBN 978-0-7534-6523-3 (PB)

Kingfisher books are available for special promotions and
premiums. For details contact: Special Markets Department,
Macmillan, 175 Fifth Ave., New York, NY 10010.

For more information, please visit www.kingfisherbooks.com

Printed in China
9 8 7 6 5 4 3 2 1
1TR/1010/WKT/UTD/140MA

Consultant: Dougal Dixon
Illustrations (including cover): Chris Forsey; Robin Boutell
(The Art Agency) 8–9; cartoons Tony Kenyon.

CONTENTS

How many dinosaurs were there?

There were many different dinosaurs. Scientists have already named about 500 kinds, and new ones are being found all the time. Some dinosaurs were big, and others were tiny. Some were fierce meat eaters, and others were gentle vegetarians that browsed on plants.

Apatosaurus
(plants)

Spinosaurus
(meat)

Iguanodon
(plants)

Styracosaurus
(plants)

Panoplosaurus
(plants)

Oviraptor
(meat)

Stygimoloch
(plants)

Dinosaurs were reptiles. Today's reptiles include lizards, crocodiles, tortoises, and snakes.

Like most other reptiles, dinosaurs lived on land and had dry, scaly skin. Most dinosaur eggs were hard and brittle, like birds' eggs.

How long ago did dinosaurs live?

Dinosaurs lived millions and millions of years ago. The first ones appeared about 230 million years ago, and the last ones we know about died out more than 65 million years ago. Compared with this, human history is just a hiccup— we've been around for only the past two million years.

Dinosaurs ruled Earth for a mind-boggling 165 million years!

Kentrosaurus
(plants)

Why was Tyrannosaurus a bigmouth?

Tyrannosaurus was a huge meat eater. At about 20 feet (6m) tall, it stood three times taller than a grizzly bear. Its mouth was huge, too—big enough to swallow you whole!

Many people think that Tyrannosaurus could have run as fast as 30 miles per hour (50km/h) when chasing a meal!

This is how big one of Tyrannosaurus's teeth was. The rough edges helped rip through skin and flesh.

Was Tyrannosaurus king of the dinosaurs?

The name *Tyrannosaurus* means "tyrant lizard"—a tyrant is a cruel king.

There may have been even bigger meat eaters than Tyrannosaurus. The tall dinosaur on the right is Deinocheirus. We have to guess what it looked like, as we've found only its arms and clawed hands. But these are bigger than a grown man, so the dinosaur may have been enormous!

Deinocheirus

The three dinosaurs on the left were closely related to Tyrannosaurus, but none of them was as big.

Carnotaurus   **Dilophosaurus**   **Ceratosaurus**

Which dinosaur attacked with switchblades?

Deinonychus was a fast and deadly killer. It had sharp teeth for biting and strong clawed hands for gripping and tearing. But its nastiest weapons were one long curved claw on each foot. When Deinonychus kicked, its slashing claw sprang forward like a switchblade.

The word *Deinonychus* means "terrible claw."

Velociraptor was similar to Deinonychus. Its name means "fast thief."

Deinonychus probably hunted in packs, attacking dinosaurs much larger than itself. African wild dogs do this today, chasing their prey until it gets tired and slows down and then closing in for the kill.

Why did Iguanodon stick its thumbs up?

Iguanodon was a huge and gentle plant eater, but its thumb claws were shaped like daggers. It may have used these spikes as secret weapons, stabbing with them when attacked.

Baryonyx was almost built into a wall! The dinosaur's bones were found in a pit where clay was being dug to make bricks.

Which dinosaur went fishing?

Baryonyx had an even bigger claw than Deinonychus—its name even means "heavy claw." Its claw was on its hand, and it used the claw to hook fish out of rivers, just as grizzly bears do today.

Which was the biggest dinosaur?

Brachiosaurus
40 feet (12m) high
74 feet (22.5m) long

Brachiosaurus was gigantic. If it were alive today, it would be able to peer over the top of a four-story building. It was so big that you would have needed to stretch up to touch its knee. And scientists have discovered bones of a long-necked dinosaur called Argentinosaurus that was even bigger!

Although Diplodocus was one of the longest dinosaurs, its head was tiny —not much bigger than a horse's head of today.

Here's how these three dinosaur giants compare with today's biggest land animal, the African elephant.

The long-necked dinosaurs are called sauropods. Their necks allowed them to eat leaves in the treetops that other dinosaurs couldn't reach.

Huge dinosaurs like Brachiosaurus may have lived to be 120 years old.

Diplodocus
85 feet (26m) long

Which was the smallest?

Compsognathus is one of the smallest dinosaurs ever found—it wasn't much bigger than a chicken. It ran on two skinny legs, hunting for small animals, such as lizards, to eat.

Apatosaurus
70 feet (21m) long

Did dinosaurs lay eggs?

Yes, dinosaurs laid eggs, just as today's reptiles do. The mothers laid them in nests on the ground. Dinosaur eggs were different sizes and shapes—some were almost round, and others were long and thin.

The biggest dinosaur egg found so far belonged to a long-necked dinosaur called Hypselosaurus. The egg is five times as long as a chicken's egg.

Baby dinosaurs had a bony horn on their nose to help them break out of their eggs.

Long-necked dinosaurs took care of their young, too. When a herd was on the move, the young walked in the middle, guarded by their huge parents.

Groups of Maiasaura nested close together, just like sea birds do today.

Which dinosaur was a good mother?

In 1978, scientists made a very exciting discovery in Montana—a complete dinosaur nesting site, with nests, eggs, and even baby dinosaurs. The dinosaurs that laid the eggs were given the name Maiasaura, which means "good mother lizard."

Could any dinosaurs swim?

Dinosaurs may have been able to swim if they wanted to cross a river, but they didn't live in the water. There were all types of other reptiles living in the oceans in dinosaur times, though—some of them even looked a little like dinosaurs.

Some turtles were huge in dinosaur times. Archelon was longer than a rowboat.

Kronosaurus

Kronosaurus was a real big-head! Its skull was more than twice the size of Tyrannosaurus's skull.

Mosasaurus
Mosasaurus was a giant sea lizard.

14

Elasmosaurus

Elasmosaurus had a long snakelike neck, similar to Diplodocus and the other sauropod dinosaurs. It probably swam holding its neck and tiny head out of the water, dropping them down suddenly to snatch passing fish.

These sea reptiles couldn't breathe underwater, as fish do. They had to come up to the surface to breathe air, just as whales and dolphins do today.

Ichthyosaurus

Ichthyosaurus looked a lot like a modern dolphin. It had sharp eyes for spotting fish to eat, and it could swim very fast to catch them.

The first whole skeleton of an ancient reptile ever found was an Ichthyosaurus's. Mary and Joseph Anning were 12 and 16 years old in 1810 when they discovered it at the foot of coastal cliffs in Dorset, southern England.

Teleosaurus

There were also sea crocodiles in dinosaur times. Teleosaurus's long snout was lined with many sharp teeth—all the better for grabbing hold of slippery fish or squids!

15

Could any dinosaurs fly?

There were many flying reptiles in dinosaur times, but as far as we know, none of them were true dinosaurs. These flying reptiles are called pterosaurs. Some were as tiny as swallows, and others were huge.

Pteranodon
Pteranodon was bigger than any flying bird today. Its crest may have helped it steer through the air.

Baby pterosaurs were probably given food by their parents in much the same way that young birds are fed today.

The pterosaur Quetzalcoatlus was the largest flying creature Earth has ever known. It was bigger than a modern hang glider.

Pterosaurs were more like bats than birds. They didn't have feathers, but most of them had soft, furry bodies like bats and leathery wings made of skin.

Dimorphodon

Dimorphodon's head looked like a modern puffin's. Its face and mouth may have been brightly colored like a puffin's, too.

Dsungaripterus

The tip of Dsungaripterus's strange mouth would have been useful for prizing sea snails and shellfish off rocks.

Pterodaustro

Pterodaustro probably used its bristly bottom jaw like a sieve to filter tiny creatures out of the water.

Why did Triceratops have horns?

Triceratops looked fierce, but it was a plant eater and more used to feeding than fighting. It used its three sharp horns to scare away hungry meat-eating dinosaurs— or, if that didn't work, to fight them!

Torosaurus had the largest head of any land animal that has ever lived. With the neck frill, its head was as long as a modern car!

There were many different kinds of dinosaurs with horns and neck frills.

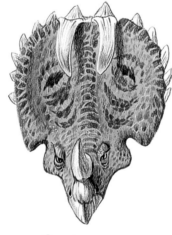

Centrosaurus

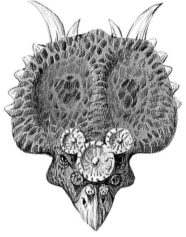

Pachyrhinosaurus

A charging Triceratops was unstoppable! It could gallop faster than a rhino, and it weighed more than a male African elephant.

Which dinosaur had body armor?

The thick, leathery skin on top of Ankylosaurus's body had hard, bony lumps and spikes growing on it. This suit of bony armor made the dinosaur into a living tank—very difficult to attack!

Ankylosaurus may have crouched down to hide its soft belly when it was attacked. Meat eaters would have broken their teeth on the armored skin on top of its body.

Chasmosaurus

Which dinosaur had a sting in its tail?

Stegosaurus didn't have horns—its deadly weapons were at the other end of its body. The long, sharp spikes on its tail weren't poisonous like bee stings, but they could still give terrible wounds.

The plates on Stegosaurus's back may have worked like solar panels, soaking up the Sun's heat and helping keep the dinosaur warm.

Ankylosaurus may have had eyelike patterns on its tail club. If a meat eater thought the club was a head, it would have had a nasty surprise!

Diplodocus's tail helped stop it from falling over when it stretched up on its back legs to feed on high branches.

Just as circus tightrope walkers use poles to help them balance, two-legged dinosaurs held their tails out straight for balance when running.

Which dinosaur used a whip?

The long-necked dinosaurs were big enough to scare off most meat eaters. But if a dinosaur like Diplodocus did have to fend off at an attacker, it could lash its long tail like a whip.

Did dinosaurs sing?

Some duck-billed dinosaurs had musical heads! Their horns and crests were hollow, like trombone pipes. Many scientists think that by blowing through their noses, duckbills may have made a loud booming noise like a foghorn.

Scientists once thought that Parasaurolophus used its long crest to breathe underwater. Unfortunately, the crest didn't have holes at the top end to let in air!

Lambeosaurus

Hypacrosaurus

Duckbills were named after their long, flat snouts, which ended in a beak like a duck's bill. The scientific name for this group is hadrosaur.

Corythosaurus

Which dinosaurs were headbangers?

Stegoceras had a strong bony skull that may have been used as a battering ram. Its skull worked like a crash helmet, protecting the soft brain inside.

Parasaurolophus

Were dinosaurs showoffs?

Many animals like to show off to one another, especially when trying to attract a mate. It's likely that some dinosaurs did, too. The duckbills may have shown off by having brightly colored and patterned crests.

Some people think that Edmontosaurus might have shown off by blowing up its forehead like a balloon.

What did dinosaurs eat?

Meat-eating dinosaurs didn't have just other dinosaurs on the menu. There were many different creatures to eat— from insects, lizards, and birds to small, furry, ratlike mammals. Vegetarian dinosaurs ate the leaves of plants and trees.

As well as teeth for chewing, vegetarian dinosaurs like Psittacosaurus had horny beaks for biting through tough plant stems.

Which dinosaurs had hundreds of teeth?

Duck-billed dinosaurs had many tiny teeth in tightly packed rows. When they ground their top and bottom jaws together, their teeth worked like vegetable graters.

Why did dinosaurs eat stones?

Some dinosaurs swallowed small stones that collected in their stomachs like marbles in a bag. These gizzard stones worked a little like teeth, helping grind down tough plant food.

Stony fossils of dinosaur droppings, with pieces of food inside them, help scientists find out what dinosaurs ate.

Which dinosaur liked eggs for breakfast?

Oviraptor had a strong beak instead of teeth, and two sharp spikes in the roof of its mouth. It may have used these spikes to crack open other dinosaurs' eggs so that it could suck out the food inside.

Oviraptor means "egg thief."

How do we know what dinosaurs looked like?

Because no one has ever seen a living dinosaur, scientists have to act like detectives. Their main clues are fossil bones, which can be used to build a skeleton. Fossils are the stony remains of animals and plants that died a very long time ago.

Putting dinosaur fossils together is a little like doing a jigsaw puzzle, and it's easy to make mistakes. When scientists first discovered a fossil Iguanodon, they thought its thumb spike went on its nose!

HOW FOSSILS FORM

1. A dead dinosaur was buried under a layer of sand or mud—perhaps after falling into a river or lake.

2. The soft parts of its body rotted away, leaving harder parts like the bones.

Once they have a skeleton, scientists can figure out how the bones supported the muscles . . .

. . . and what the dinosaur looked like when its muscles were covered in skin.

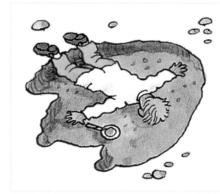

Scientists can figure out a dinosaur's weight and speed by measuring how deep its fossil footprints are and how far apart they are.

What color were dinosaurs?

3. Over millions of years, these parts turned to stone.

No one knows what color dinosaurs were. We have fossils of their skin, but these only show that it was scaly.

How are dinosaur fossils found?

Dinosaur fossils are usually buried inside rock, so they have to be dug out. People sometimes stumble across them by accident, but most fossils are found by scientists who go looking in likely places. This is easier than it sounds because only some kinds of rocks have dinosaur fossils in them.

One of the first jobs is to make a map of the digging area. Then, each time a fossil is found, it can be marked on the map.

Fossils are usually found in sandstone, clay, limestone, or shale rocks.

Dinosaurs are sometimes named after the people who found them.

It may take weeks, months, or even years to dig out a complete skeleton.

Photographs show exactly how a piece of bone was lying. This can help scientists when they put the skeleton back together again.

The finds often have to be carried away by truck over rough, bumpy ground.

Covering a fossil in a thick layer of hard plaster helps keep it safe from knocks. It's just like putting a plaster cast around a broken leg.

Dinosaur digs are often in wild places, far from any town or road. The team has to live in tents or trailers.

Where are dinosaurs found?

Dinosaurs lived all over the world. Their fossils have been found in places as far apart as the U.S. and China, England and Australia— even Antarctica!

What happened to the dinosaurs?

Something very strange happened 65 million years ago. All the dinosaurs vanished, together with all the flying reptiles and most of the sea reptiles. No one knows for sure what happened to them.

Many scientists think that giant rocks from outer space crashed into Earth, throwing up huge clouds of dust that blocked out the Sun. This changed the weather and killed off most plants. First the plant-eating dinosaurs died of cold and hunger, then the meat eaters.

Archaeopteryx looked like a dinosaur with feathers. It lived 140 million years ago, and it is the oldest bird we know about. It was a very strange bird, however, because it had a tail, clawed fingers, and teeth, just like a dinosaur.

Are there any dinosaurs around today?

Although there aren't any true dinosaurs alive today, we do have some of their relatives. Scientists have figured out that birds developed from dinosaurs, because their skeletons are so similar. So look carefully the next time you see a bird nesting in a tree or hopping across the grass!

31

Index

TITLES IN THE **I WONDER WHY** SERIES

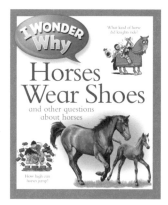

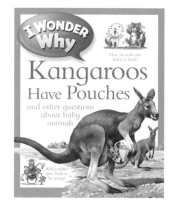

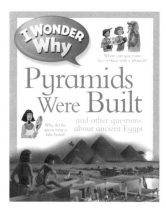

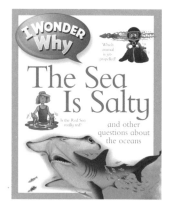

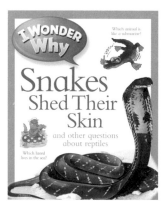

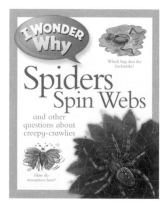

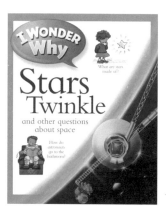

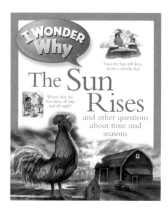

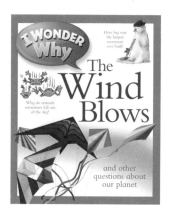